Secret Identity CHRIS BONDANTE

Oscar Takes Larry to the Moon ROBYN STOUTENBERG

No one appreciates the very special genius

of your conversation as a dog does.

CHRISTOPHER MORELY

If you pick up a dog and make

him prosperous he will not bite you.

This is the principal difference

between a dog and a man.

MARK TWAIN, FROM *Pudd'nhead Wilson*

Old Woman and Dogs ROBIN SCHWARTZ

There is no doubt that every healthy, normal boy . . . should own

a dog at some time in his life, preferably between the ages of 45 and 50.

ROBERT BENCHLEY

Jason with Portrait of Dorges GAYLORD HERRON

New City, New York LEE FRIEDLANDER

A Dog

I am alone

Someone is raking leaves

Outside

And there is one yellow leaf

On the black branch

Brushing the window.

Suddenly a wet cold nose

Nuzzles

My empty hand.

CHARLOTTE ZOLOTOW

The more I see of men, the better I like my dog.

FREDERICK THE GREAT

Happy Dog MELISSA LEE HARRIS

Poodle ROBIN SCHWARTZ

If a dog
will not come to you
after he has looked you
in the face, you ought to
go home and examine
your conscience.

WOODROW WILSON

Old dog lay in the summer sun
Much too lazy to rise and run.
He flapped an ear
At a buzzing fly.
He winked a half-open
Sleepy eye.
He scratched himself
On an itching spot,
As he dozed on the porch
Where the sun was hot.
He wimpered a bit
From force of habit,
While he lazily dreamed
Of chasing a rabbit.
But Old Dog happily lay in the sun
Much too lazy to rise and run.

James S. Tippet

Untitled Margaret Moulton

If dogs could talk, perhaps we would

find it as hard to get along with them

as we do with people.

KAREL CAPEK

nna and Luke LEE FRIEDLANDER

In moments of great joy, we all wish we had a tail to wag.
W.H. AUDEN

Dog Kissing Boy H. ARMSTRONG ROBERTS

BookCards™ is a registered trademark of Chronicle Books.

Edited by Margaret Moulton
Coordinated by Debra Lande
Design by Earl Office

Printed in Singapore.

ISBN: 0-8118-0422-4

Distributed in Canada by Raincoast Books,
112 East Third Avenue, Vancouver, B.C. V5T 1 C8

10 9 8 7 6 5 4 3 2 1

Chronicle Books
275 Fifth Street
San Francisco, CA 94103